Colour the sets.

2   Colour the sets.

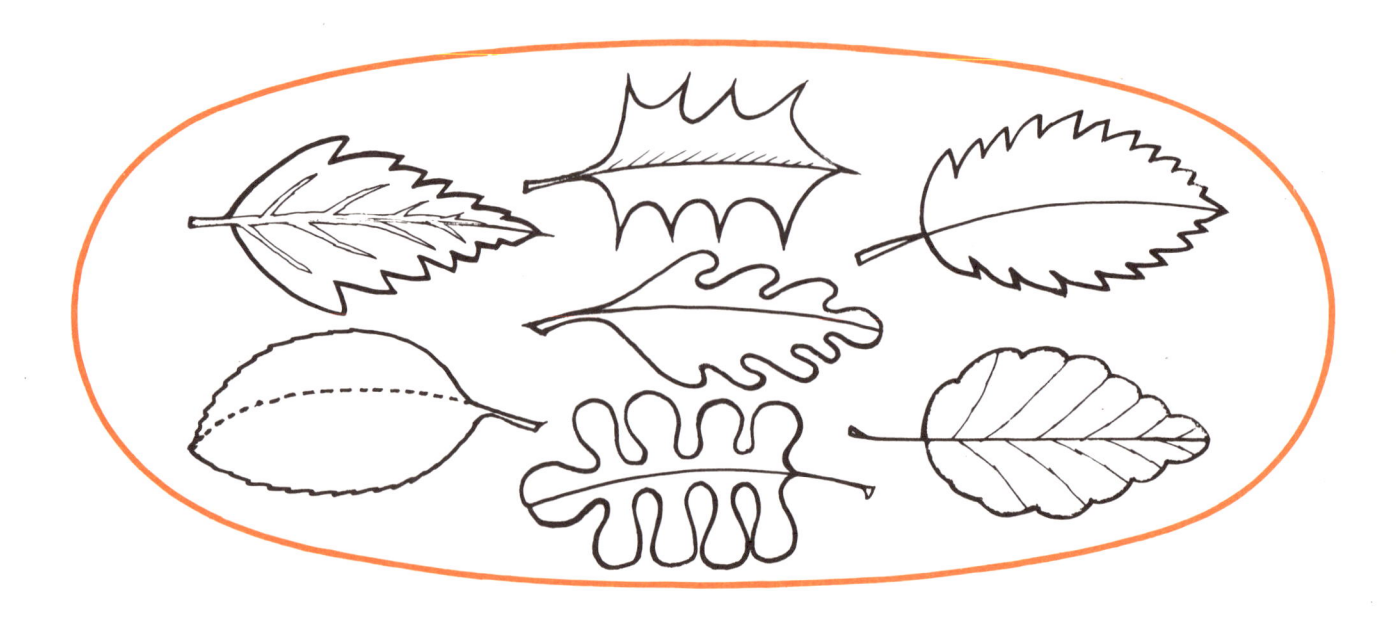

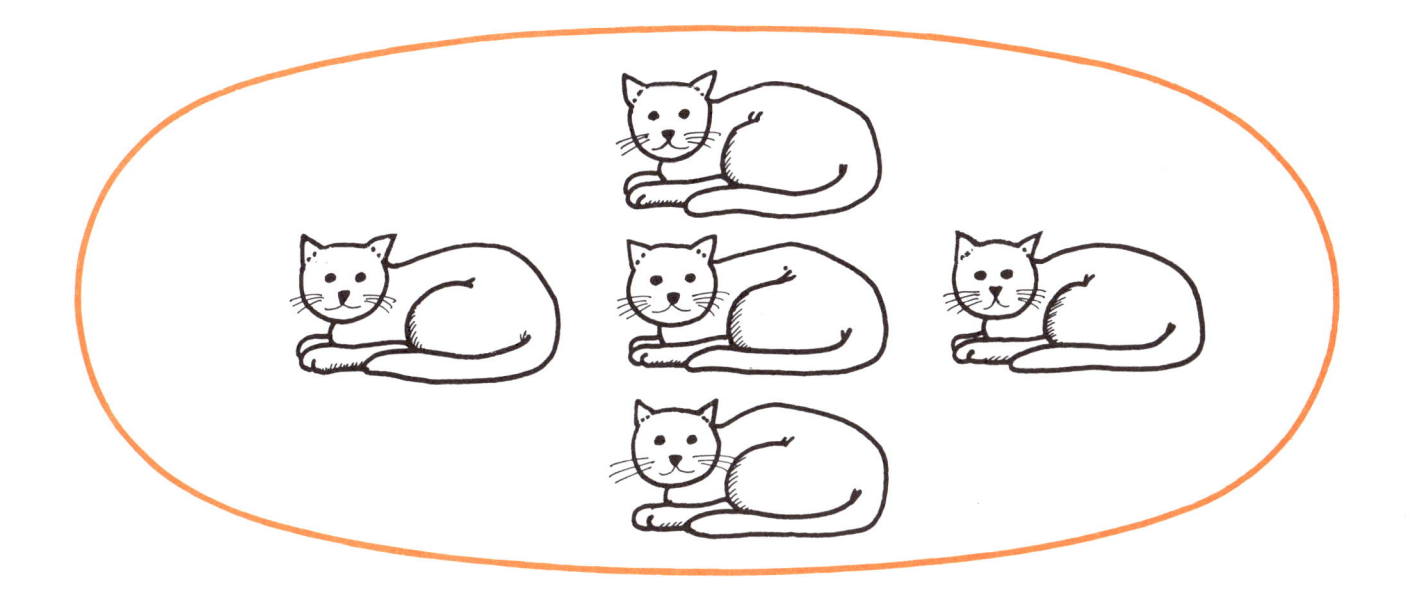

Colour the sets. 3

4   Colour the picture that belongs to the set.

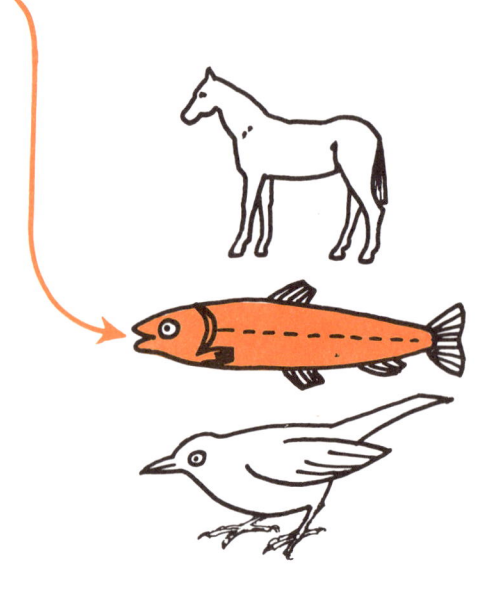

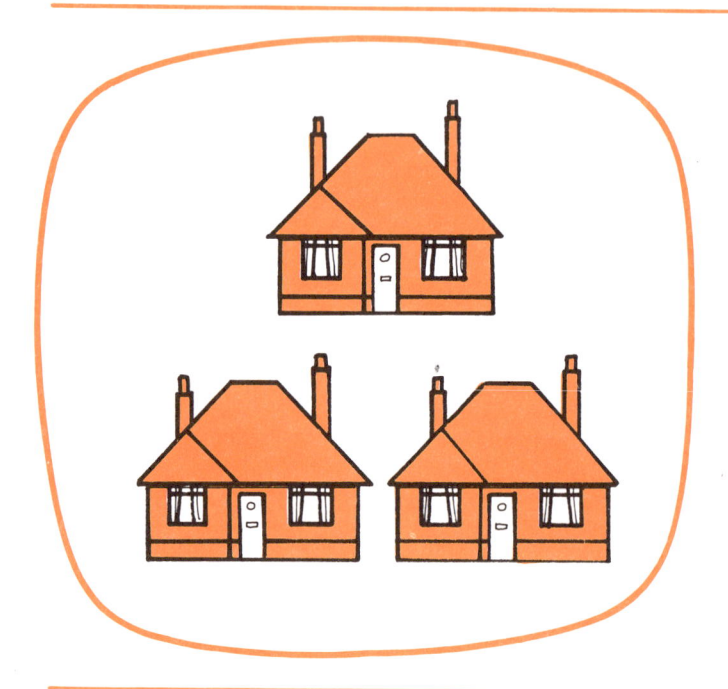

Colour the picture that belongs to the set.

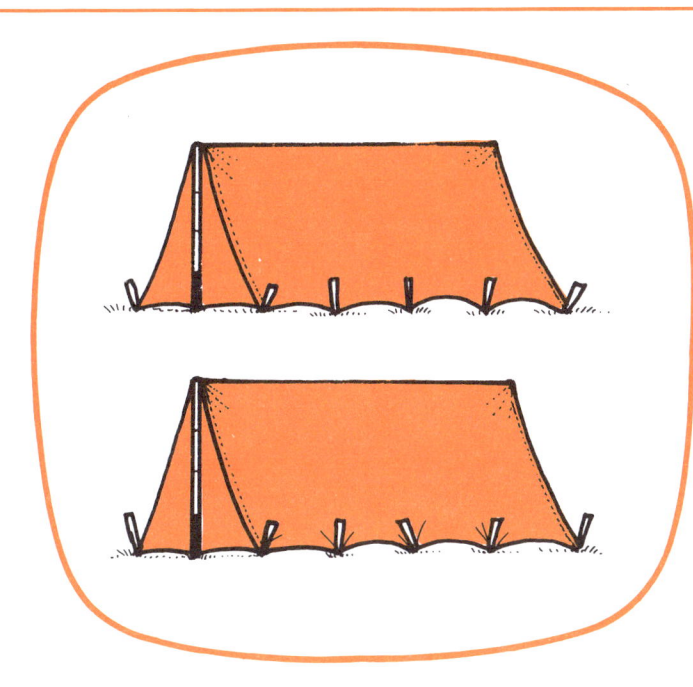

6   Add one more to each set.

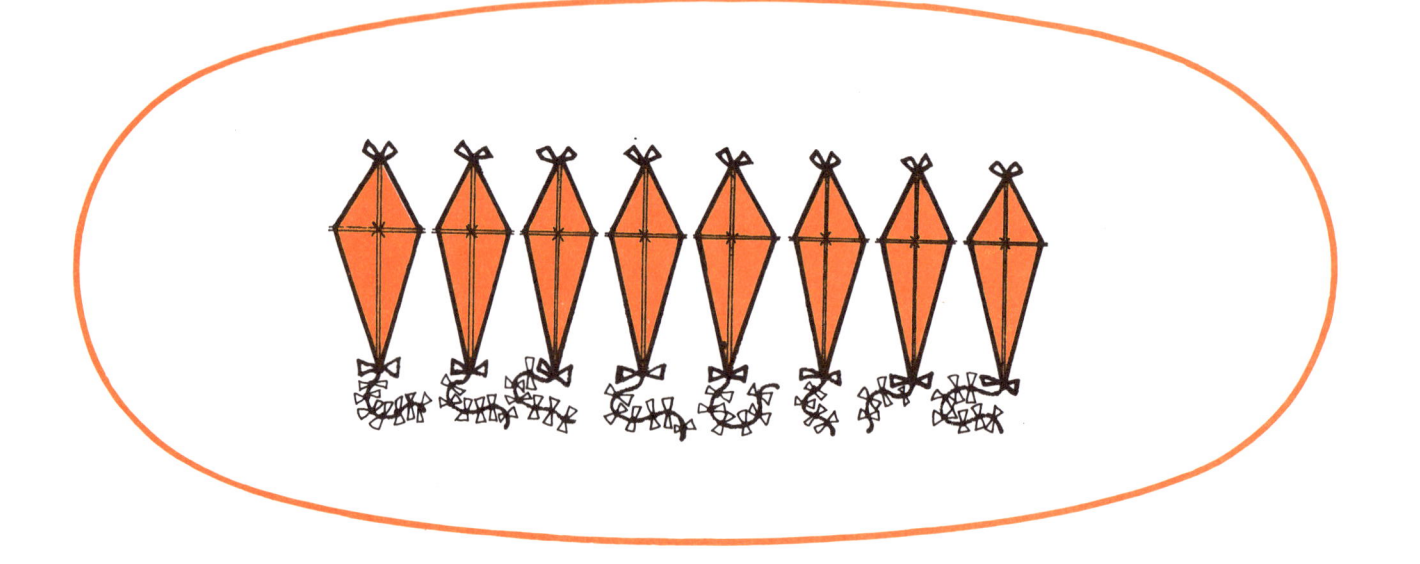

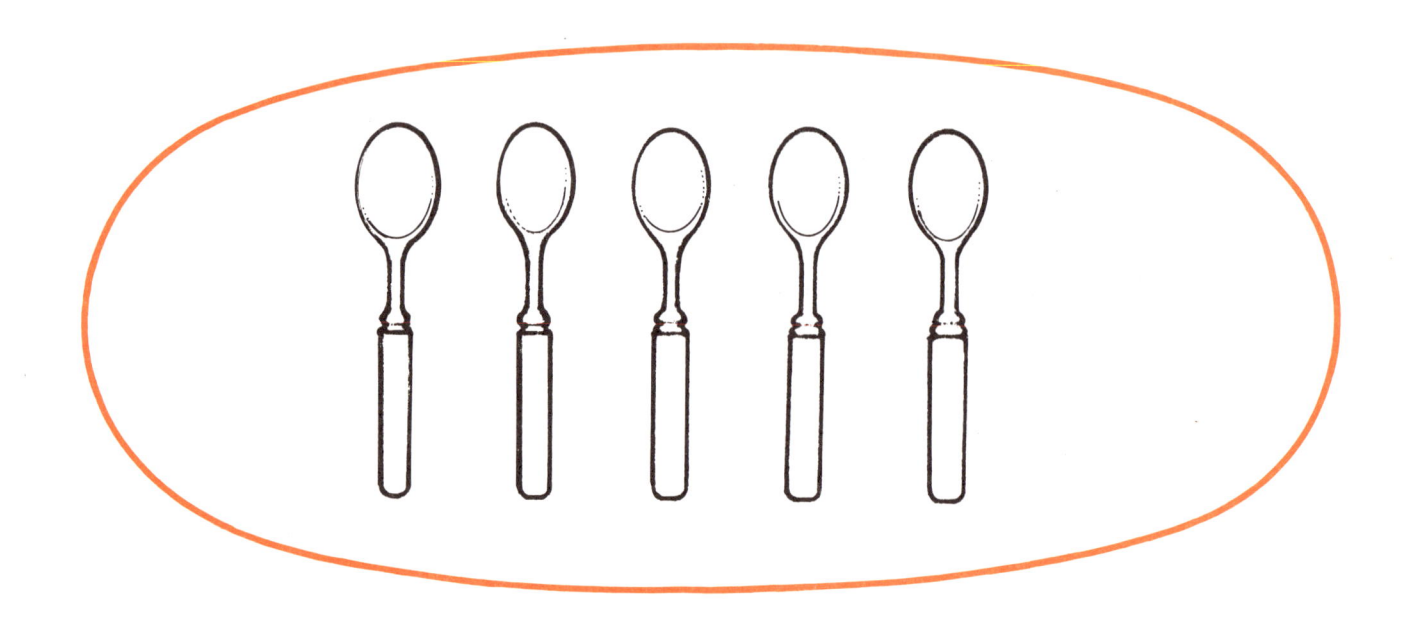

Add one more to each set. 7

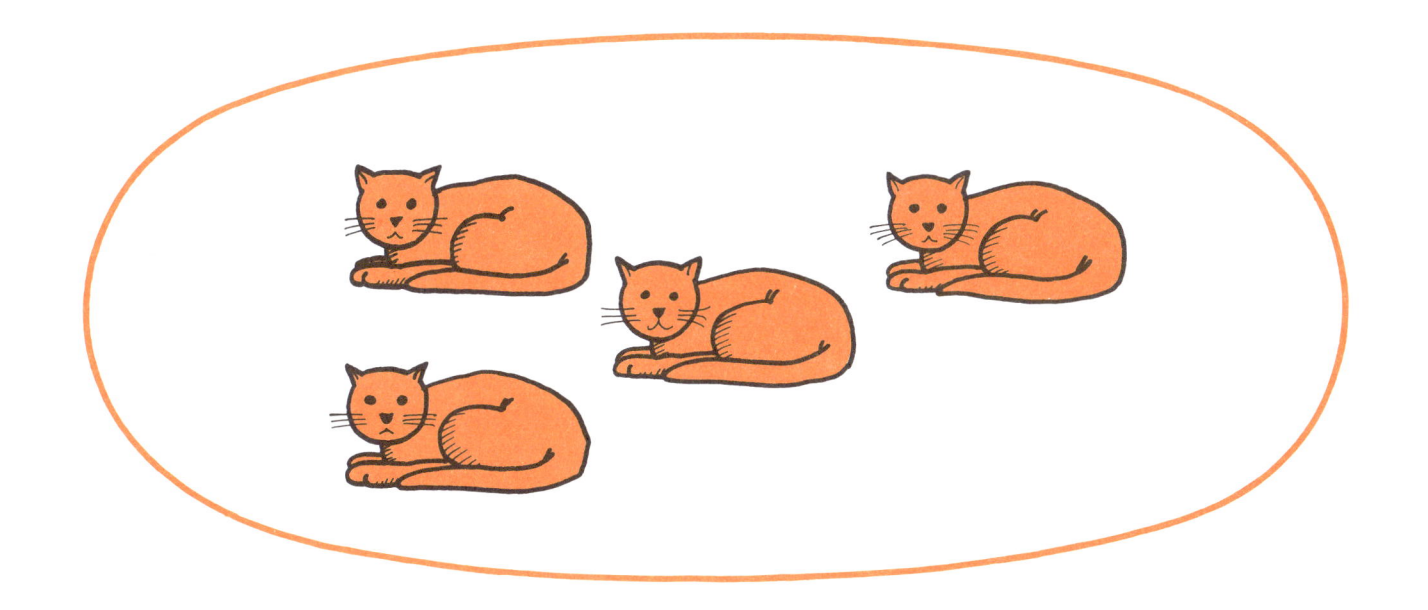

8   **Draw the sets.**

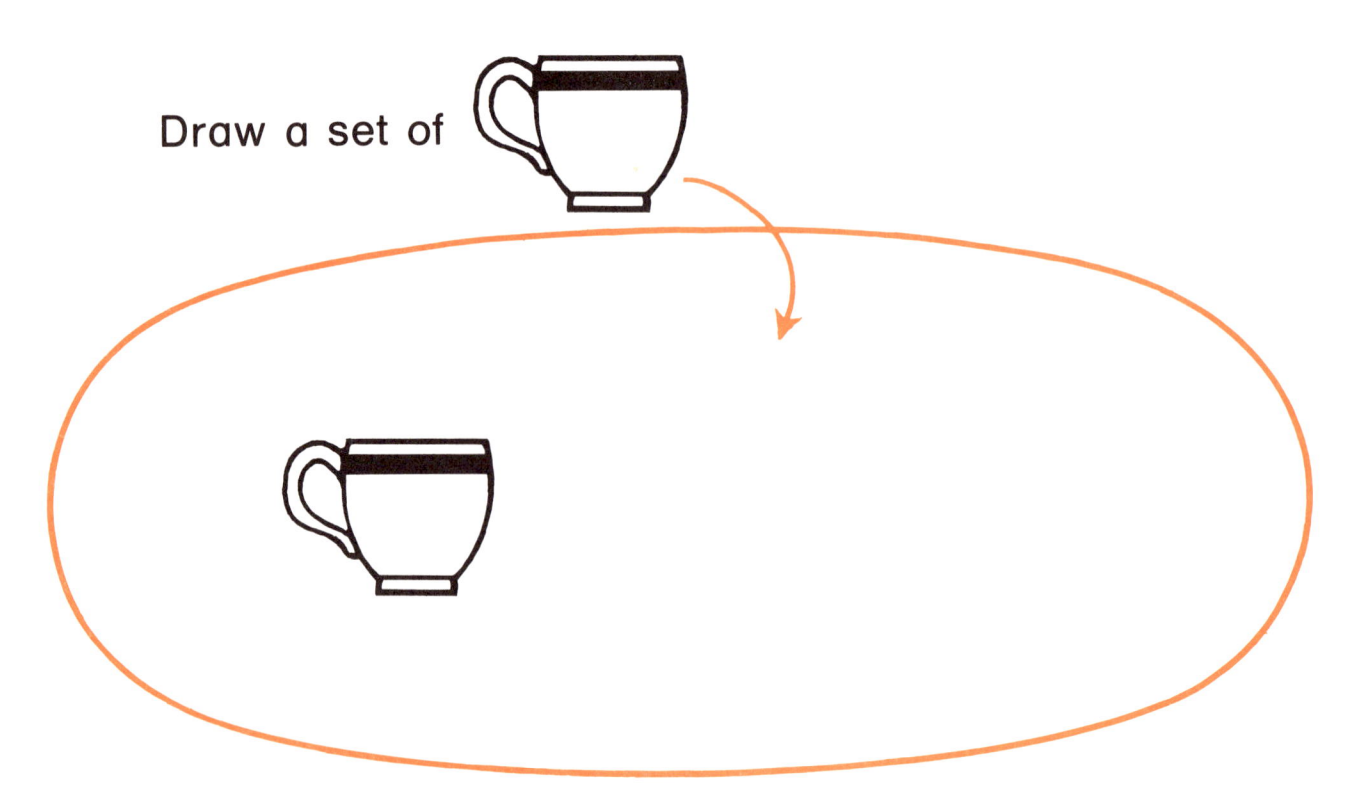

Draw a set of 🍵

Draw a set of 🦆

Draw the sets.

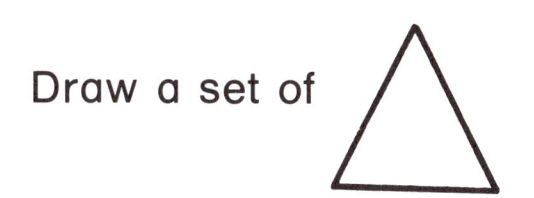

9

Draw a set of 🐱

Draw a set of △

10   Colours the sets.

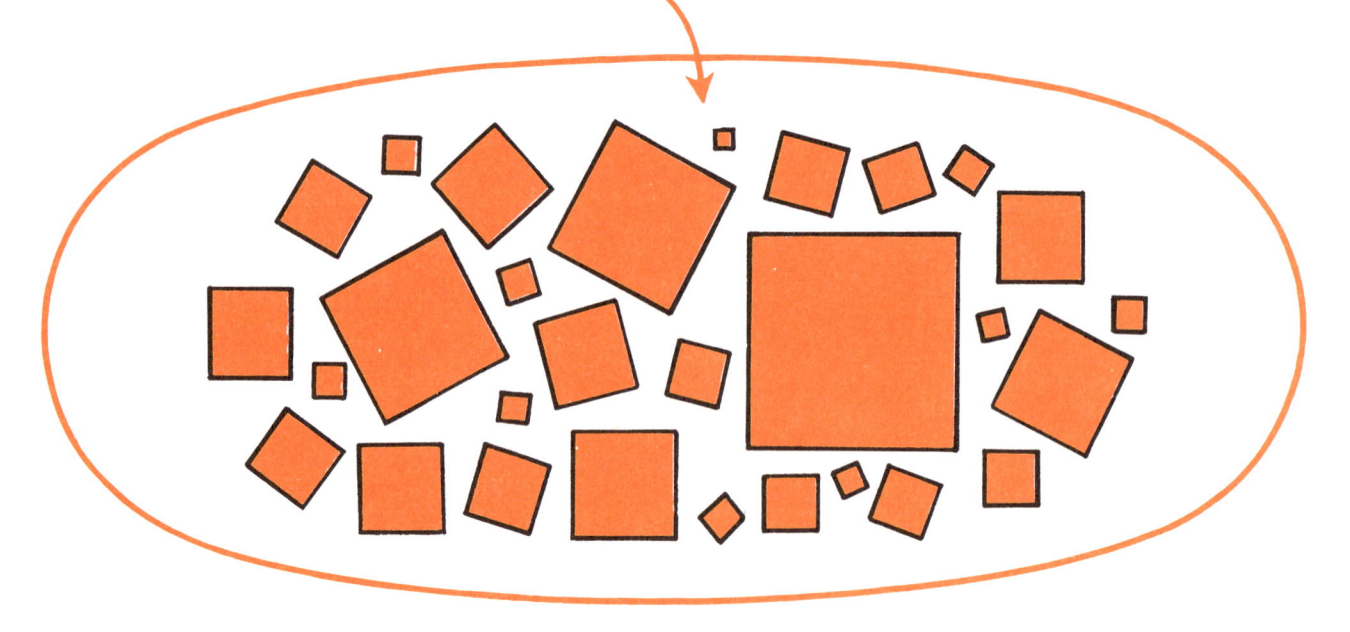

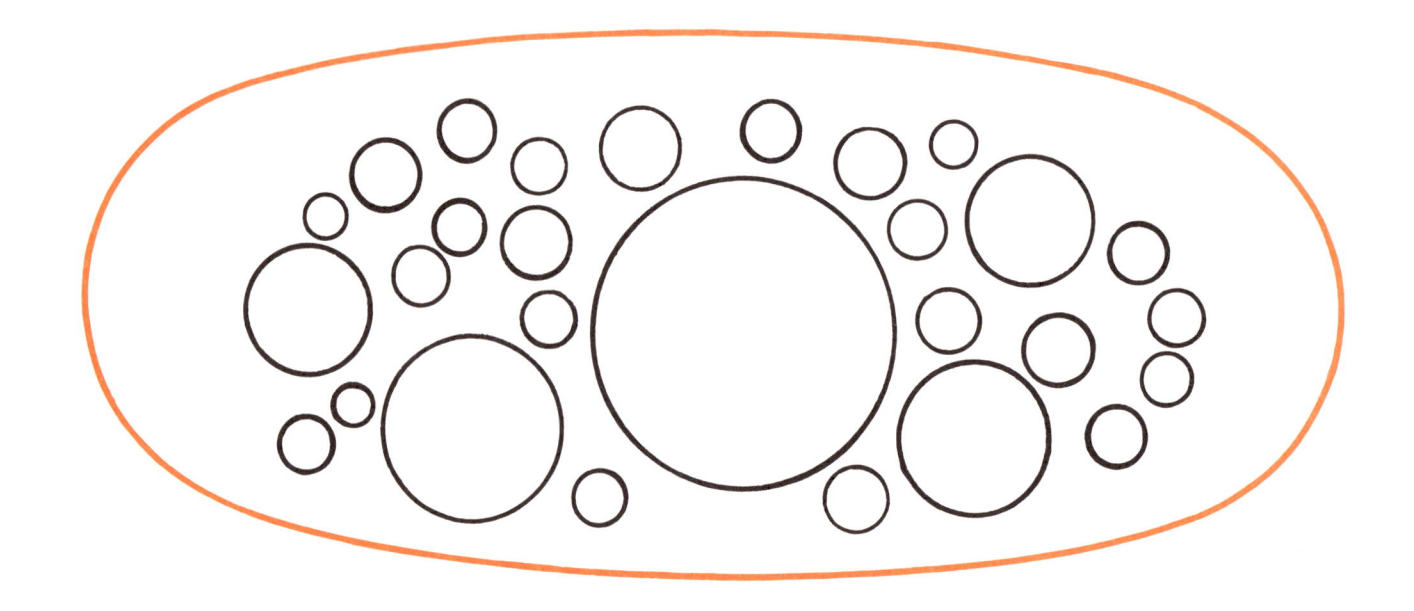

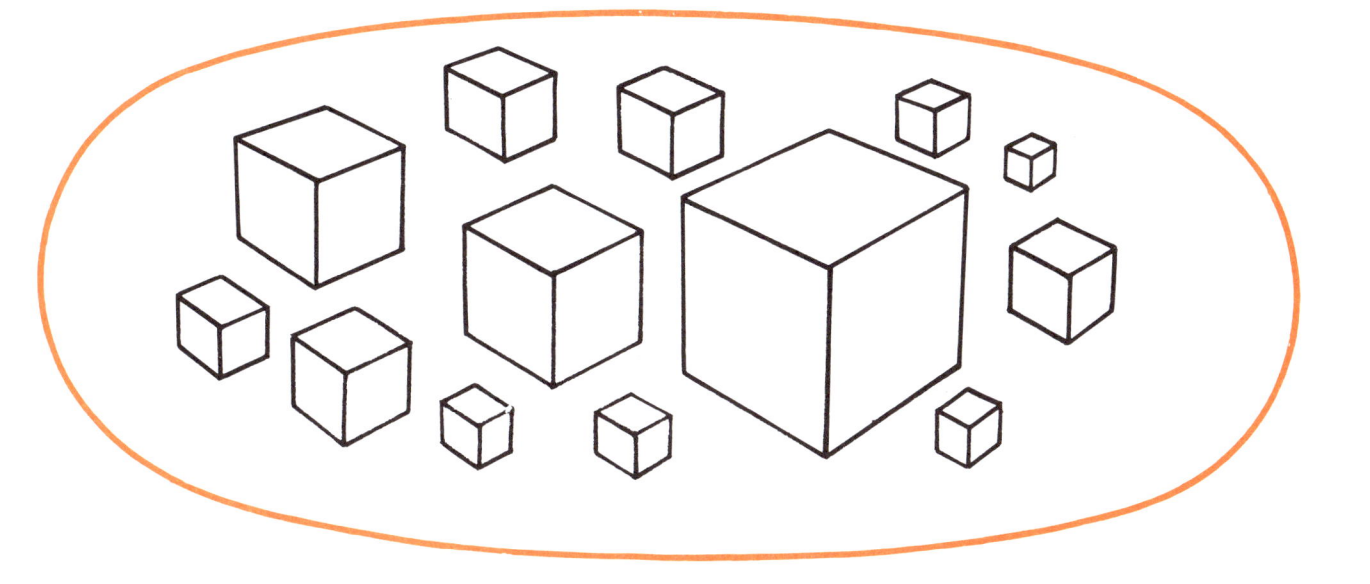

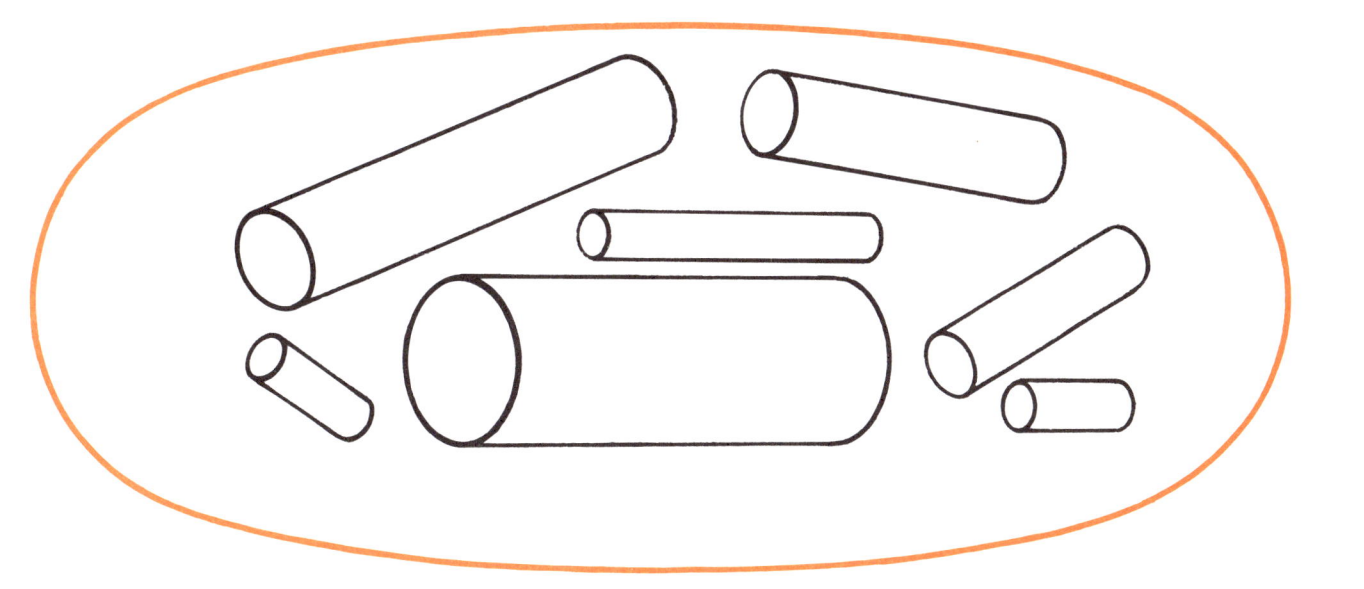

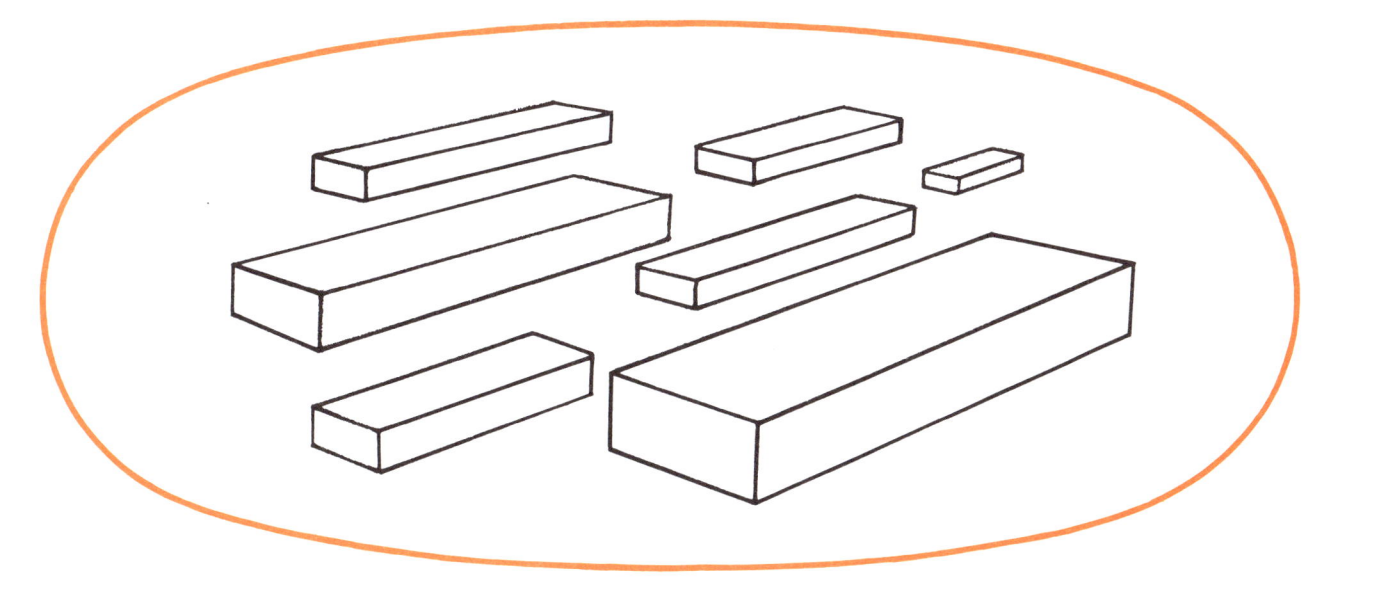

Colour the sets.

11

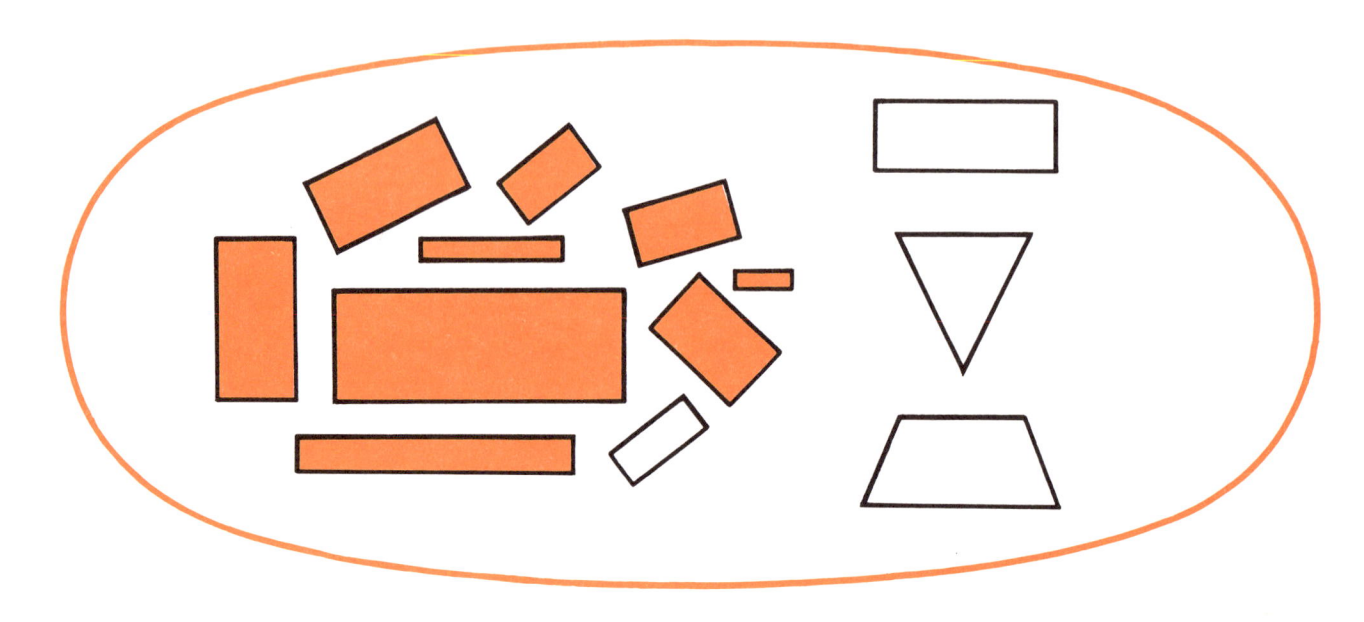

12 Colour the shape that belongs to the set.

Colour the shape that belongs to the set.

13

14   Make two sets each time.

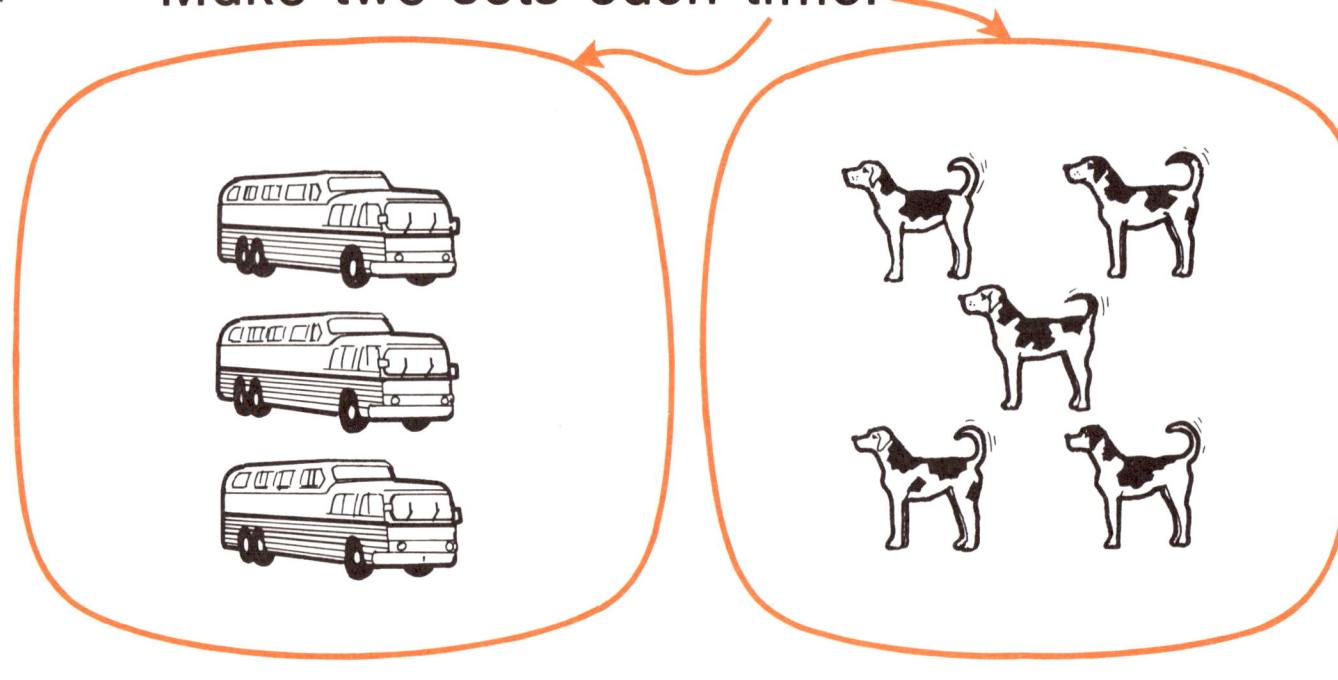

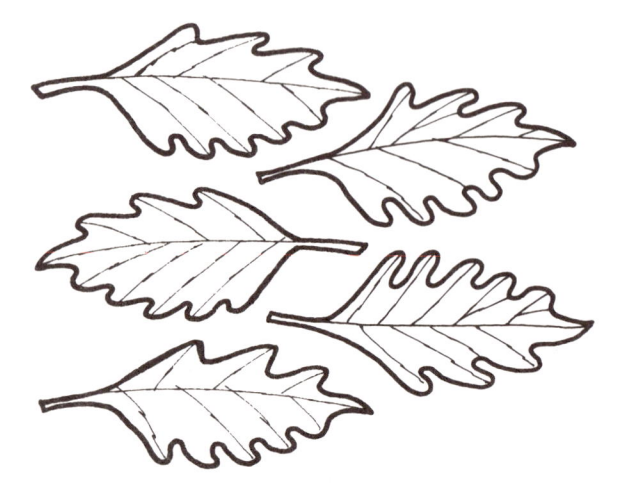

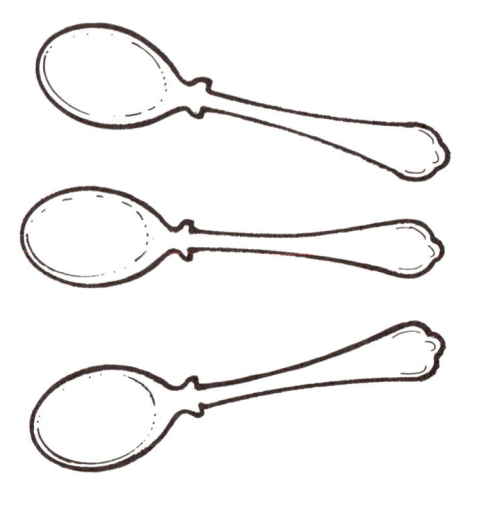

Make two sets each time.

15

16   **Make two sets each time.**

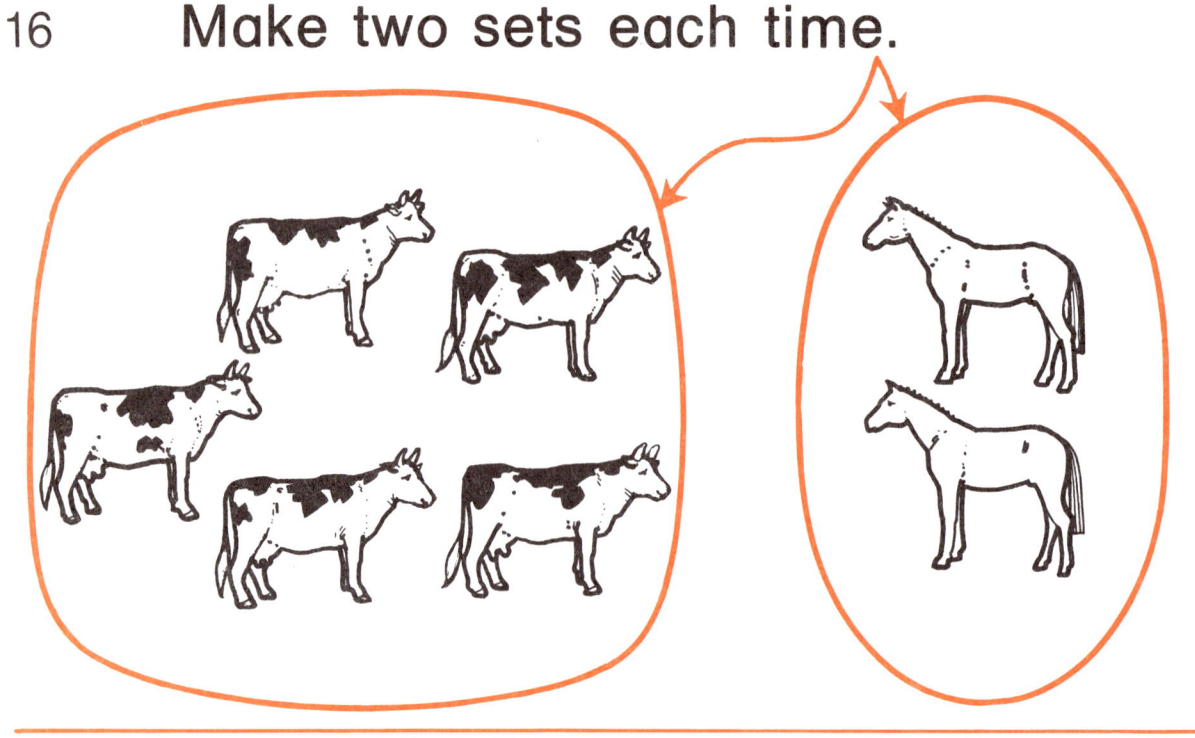

Make two sets each time.

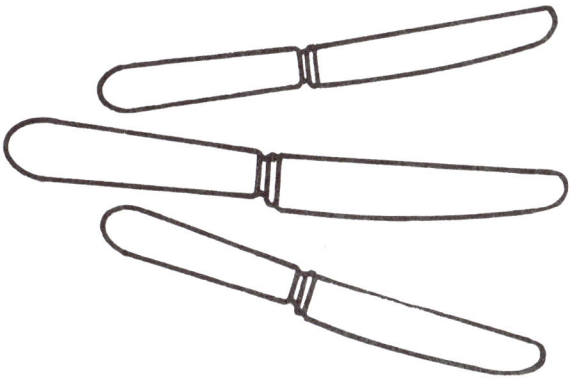

17

18 Are there enough? Write Yes or No.

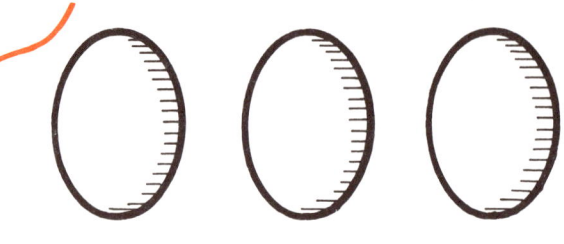

Are there enough eggs?

Yes

Are there enough drivers?

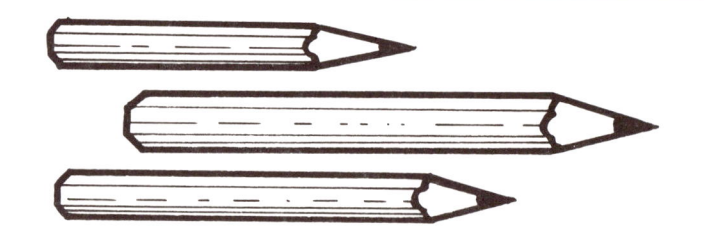

No

Are there enough pencils?

Are there enough cushions?

Are there enough? Write Yes or No.

Are there enough straws?

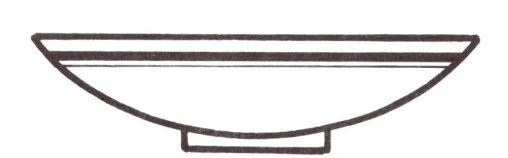

Are there enough saucers?

Are there enough lids?

Are there enough bikes?

20   Are there enough? Write Yes or No.

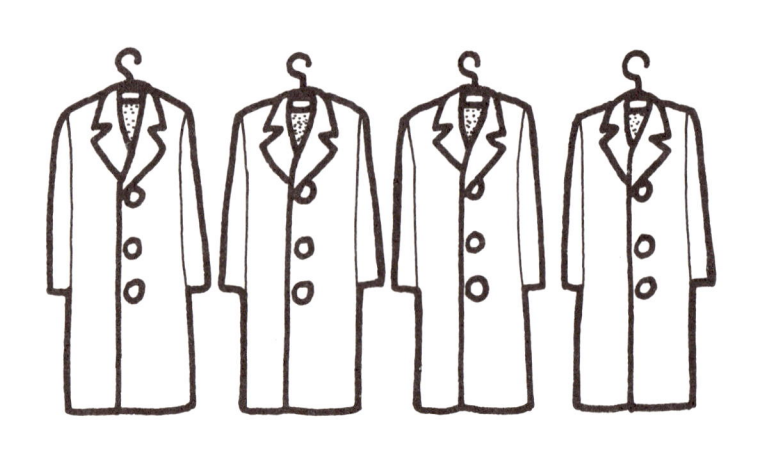

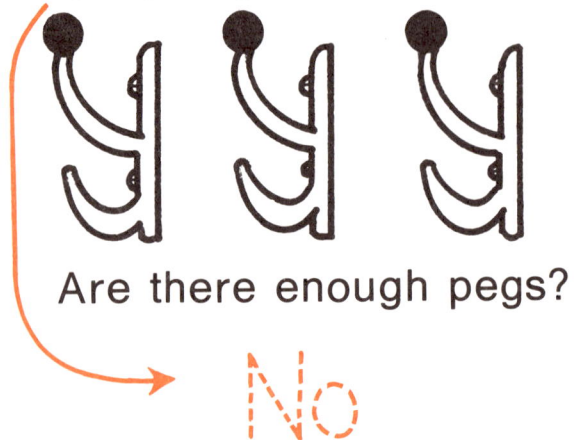

Are there enough pegs?

No

Are there enough chairs?

Yes

Are there enough corks?

Are there enough hats?

Are there enough? Write Yes or No.

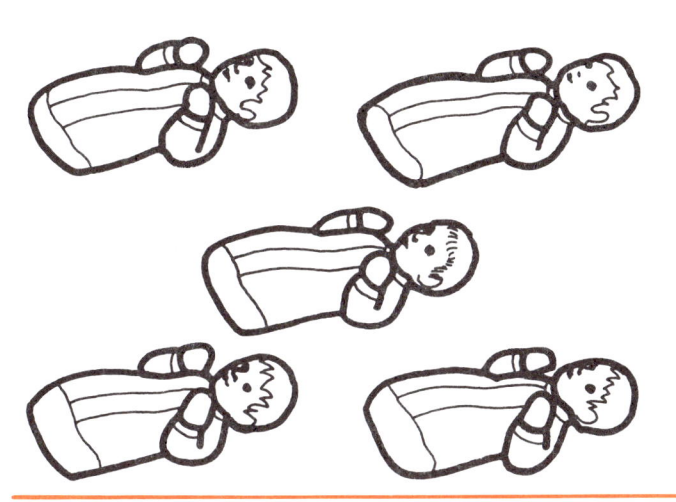

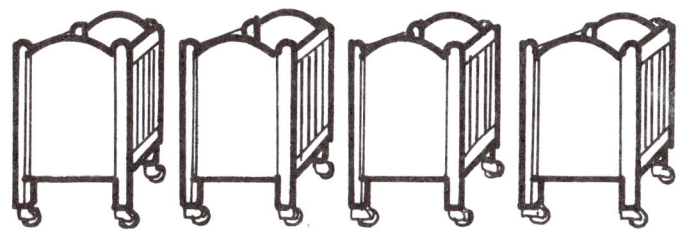

Are there enough cots?

Are there enough toothbrushes?

Are there enough horses?

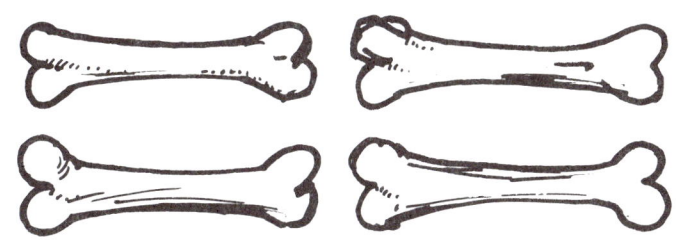

Are there enough bones?

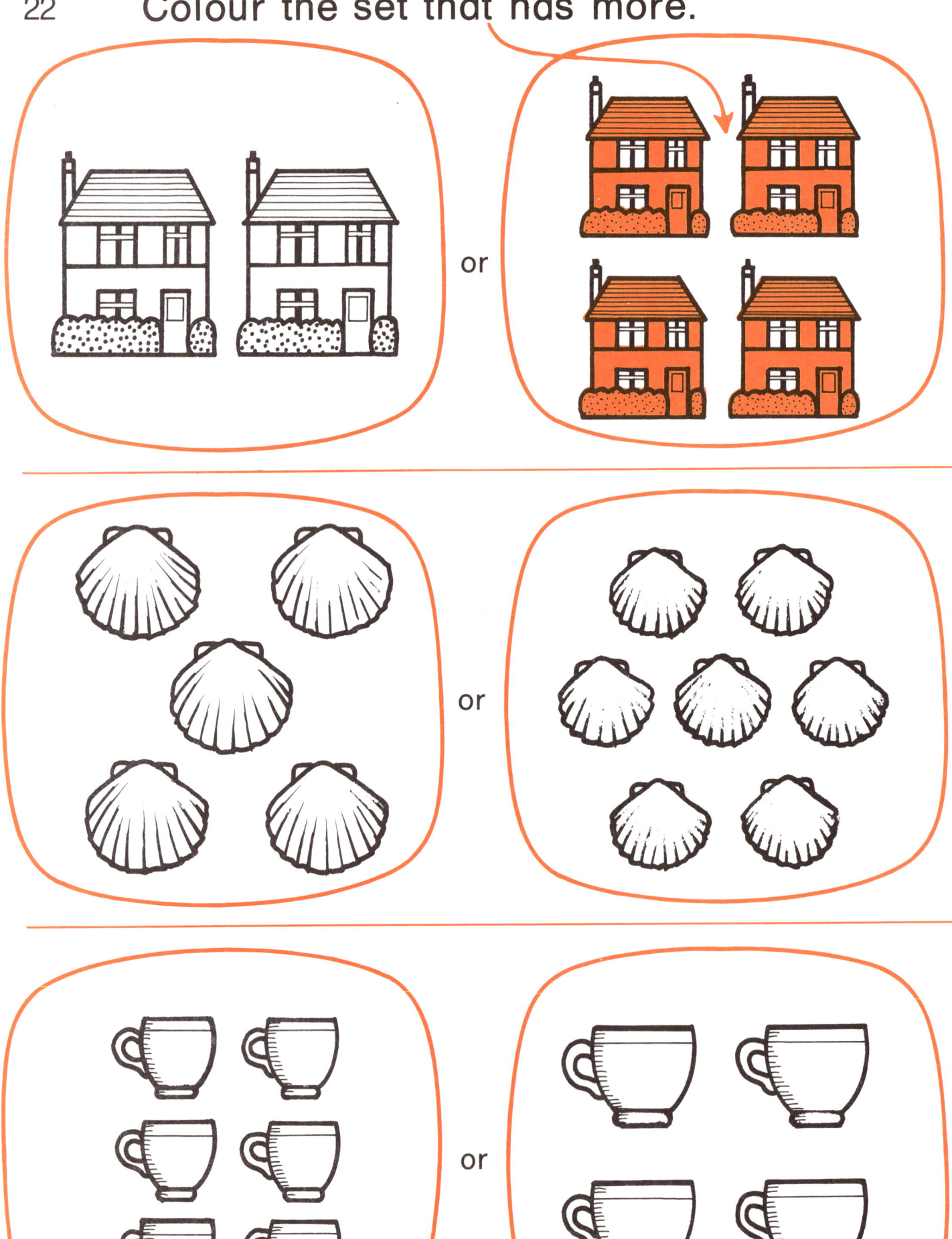

22 Colour the set that has more.

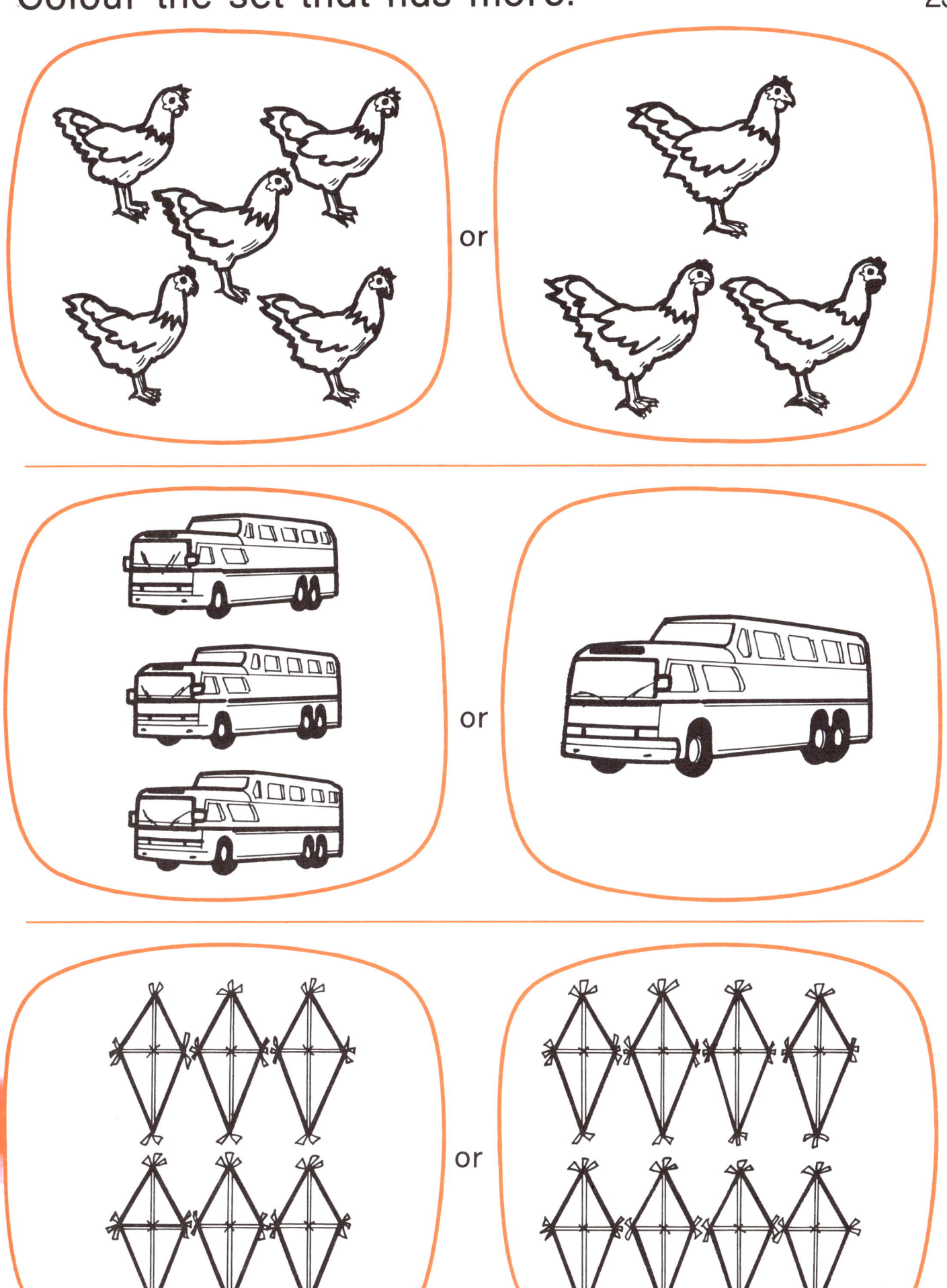

Colour the set that has more. 23

or

or

or

24   Colour the set that has more.

Colour the set that has more.

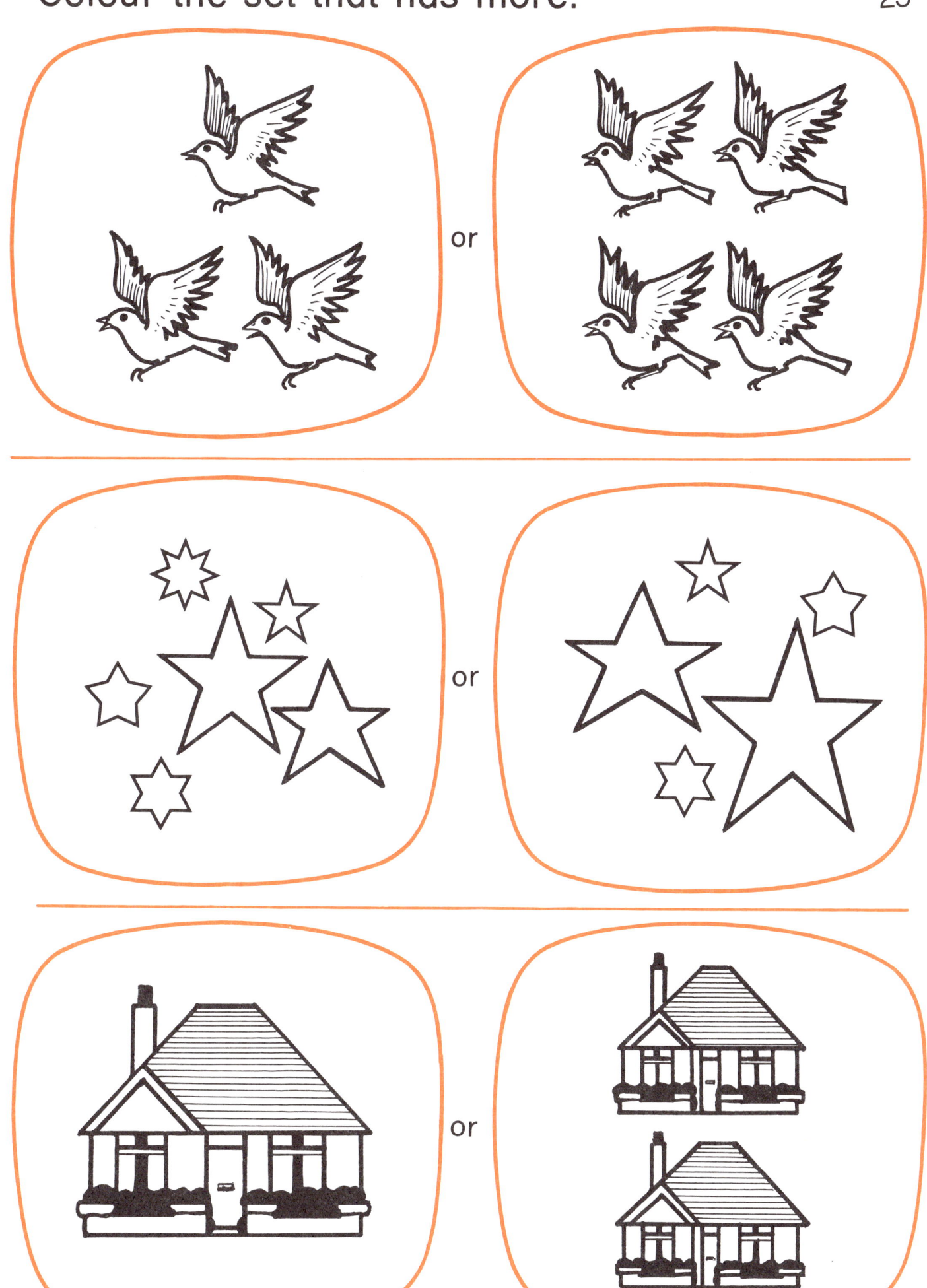

26 Colour the sets.

Colour the sets.

27

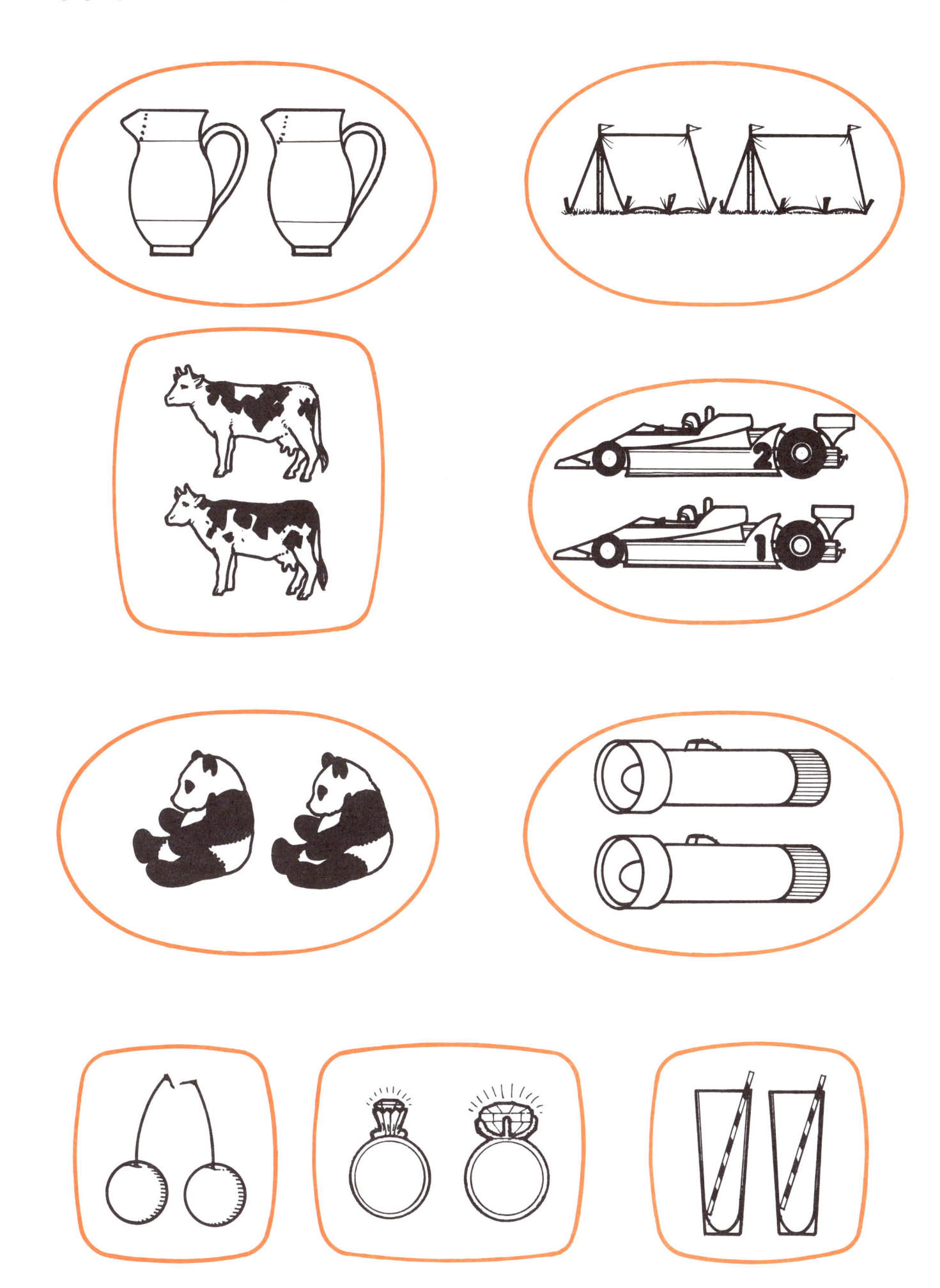

28 Ring the sets.   There are two (2) members in each.

Ring the sets.
There are two (2) members in each.

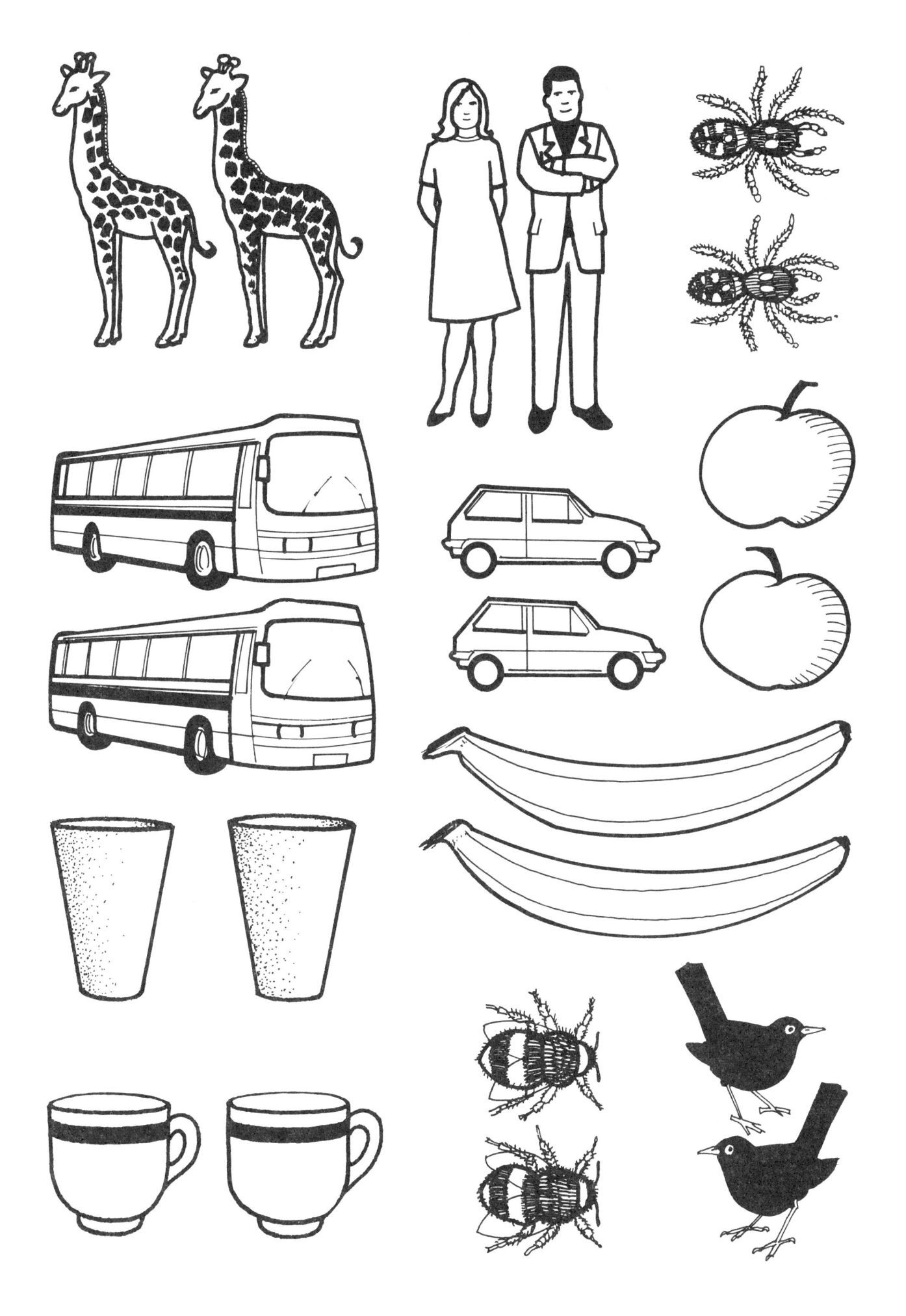

29

30 Colour the sets that have two (2) members.

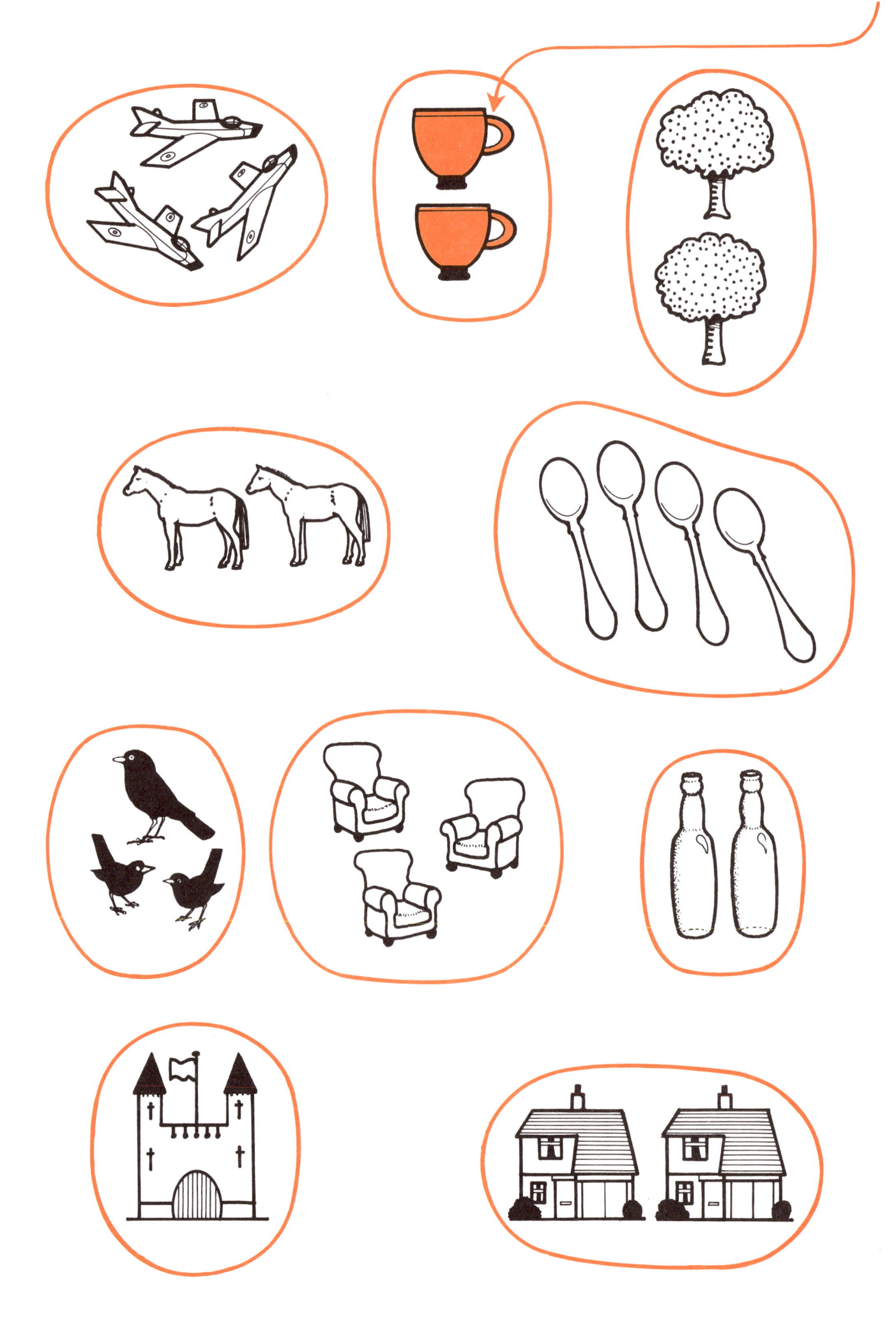

Colour the sets that have two (2) members. 31

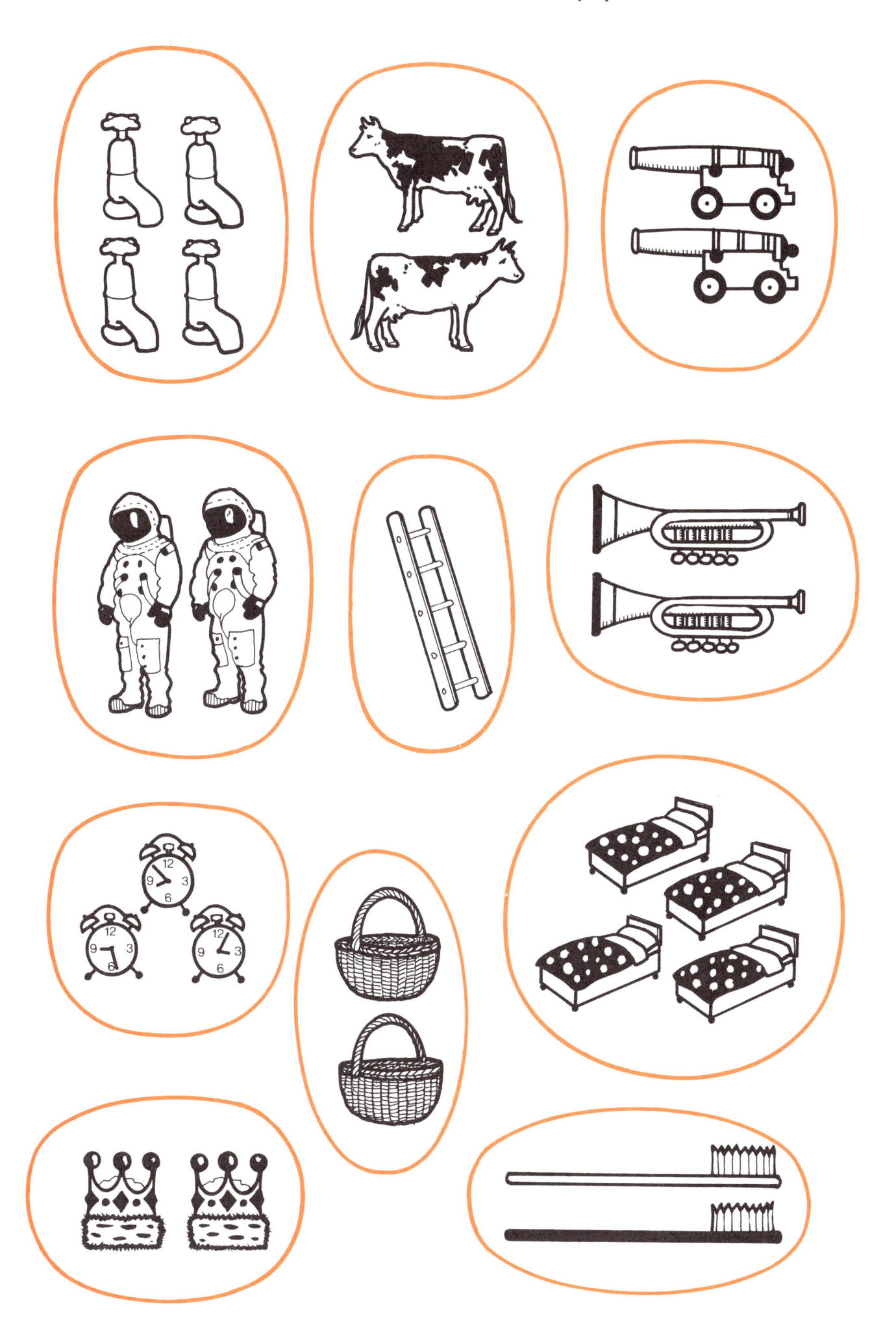

32   Make each set into a set of two (2).

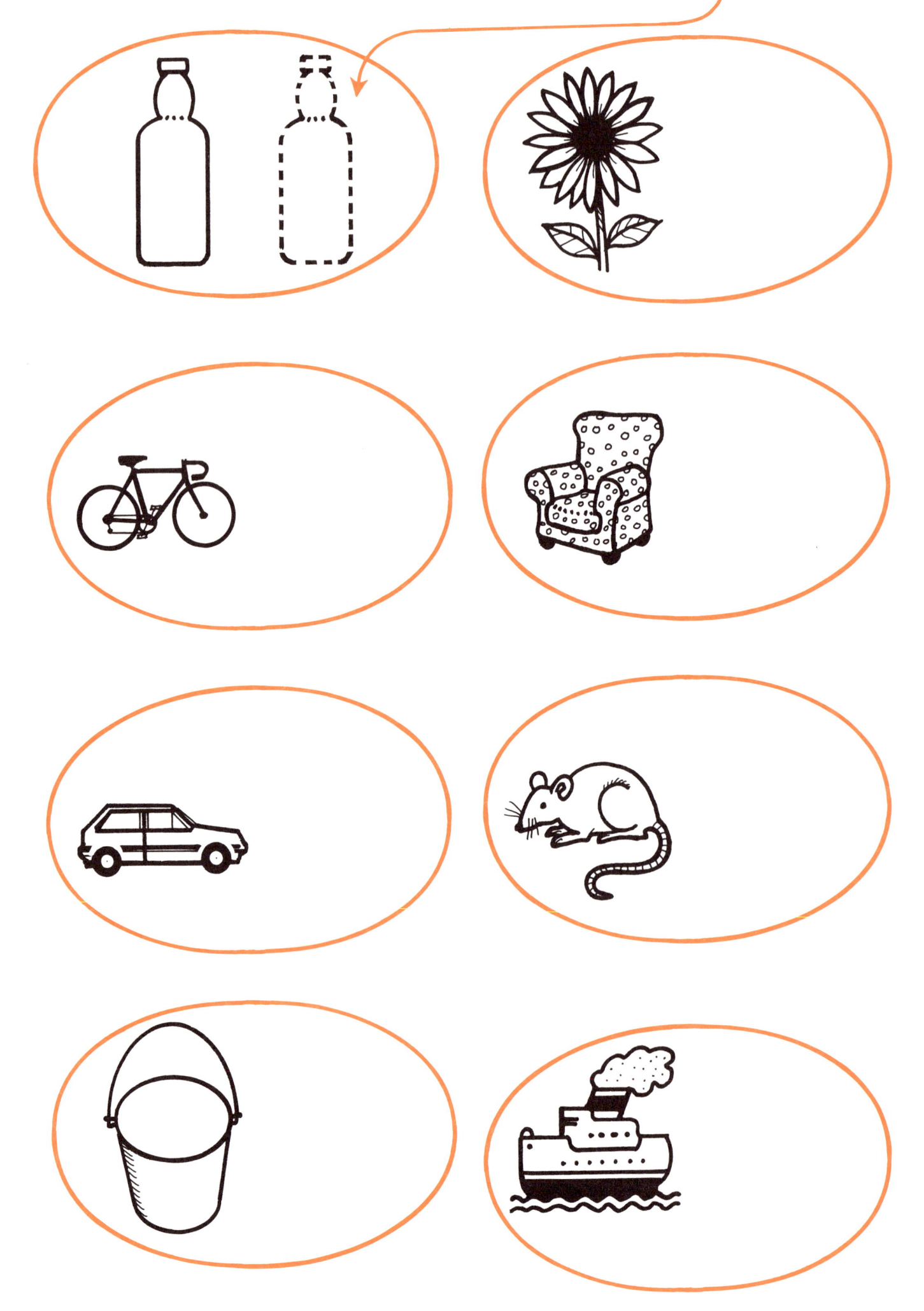

Make each set into a set of two (2).

34   Colour the sets. Write the numerals.

Write the words.

2

two

2

two

2

two

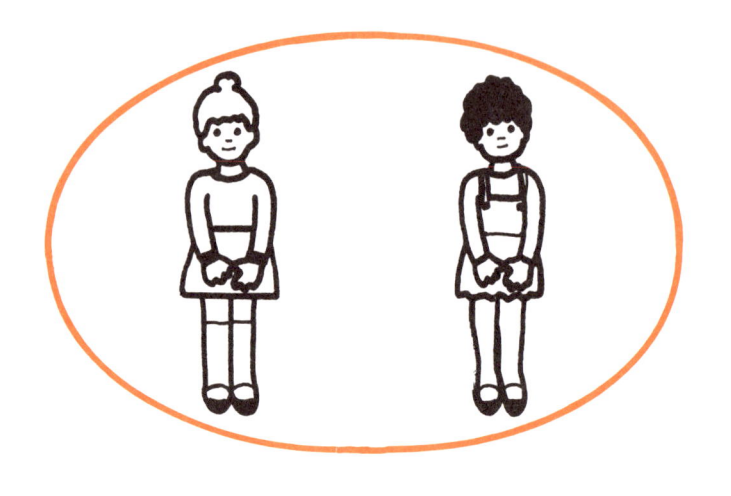

2

two

Colour the sets. Write the numerals. 35

Write the words.

2

two

2

two

36 Colour the sets.

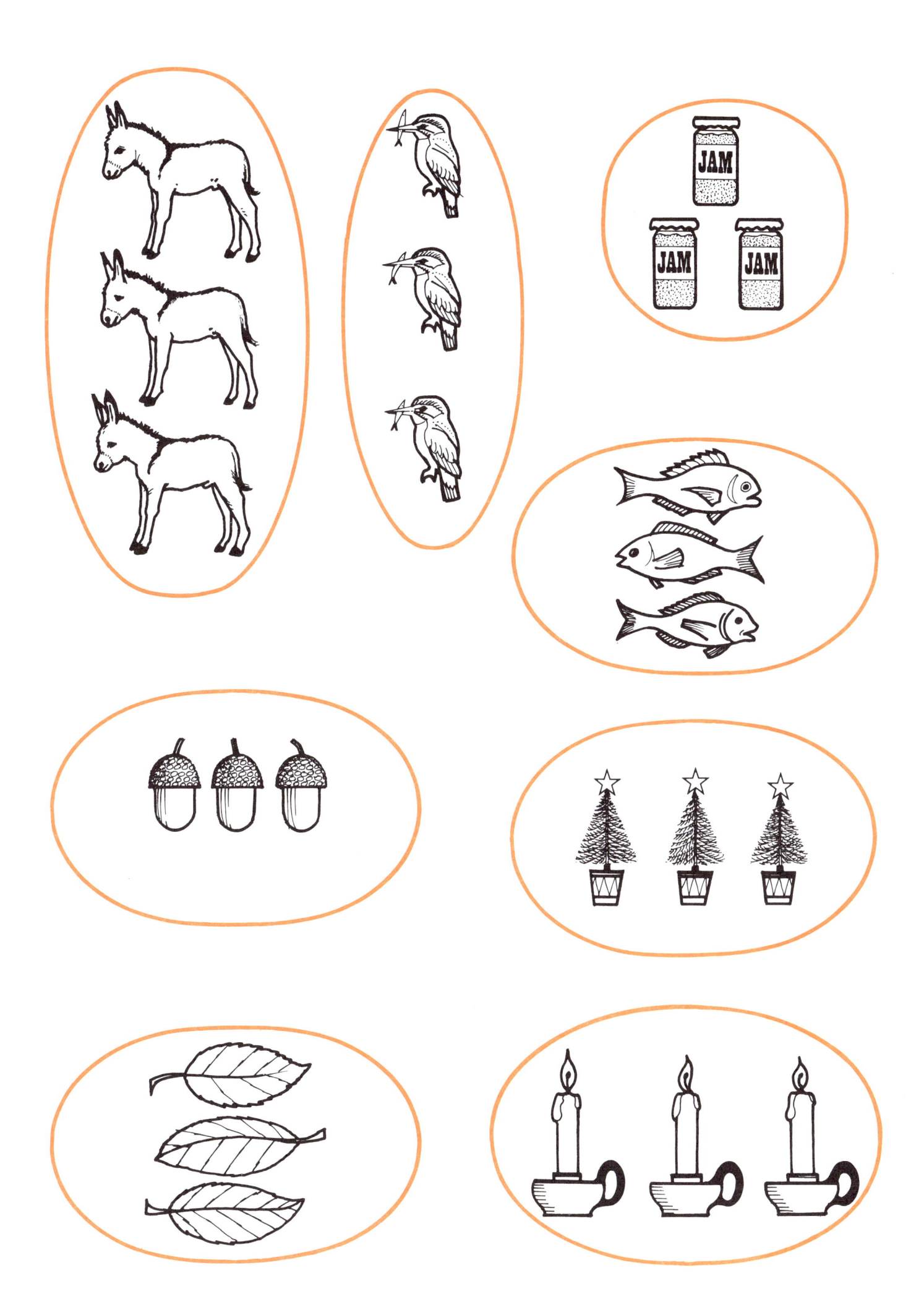

Colour the sets.

37

38 Ring the sets.
There are three (3) members in each.

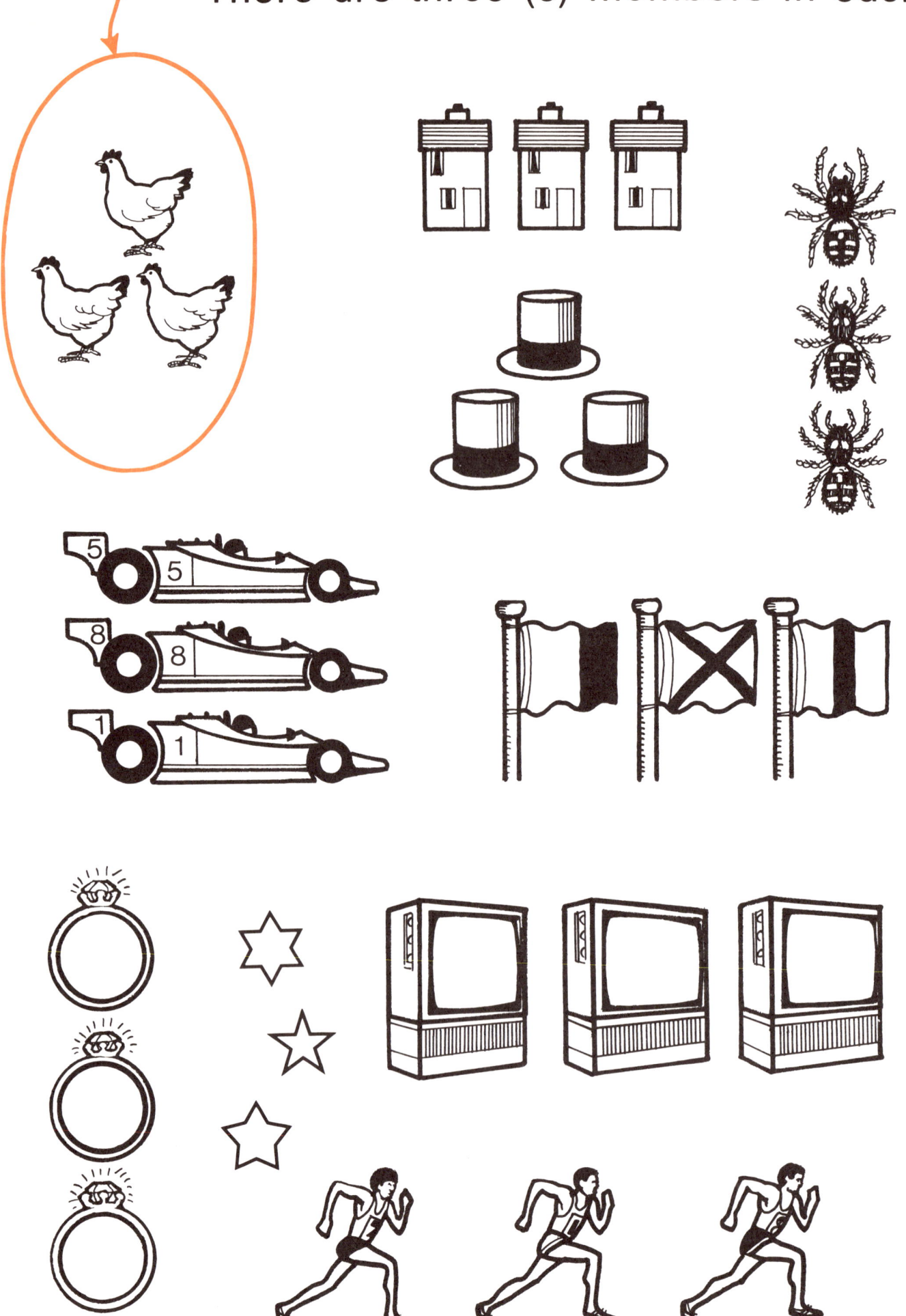

Ring the sets.
There are three (3) members in each.

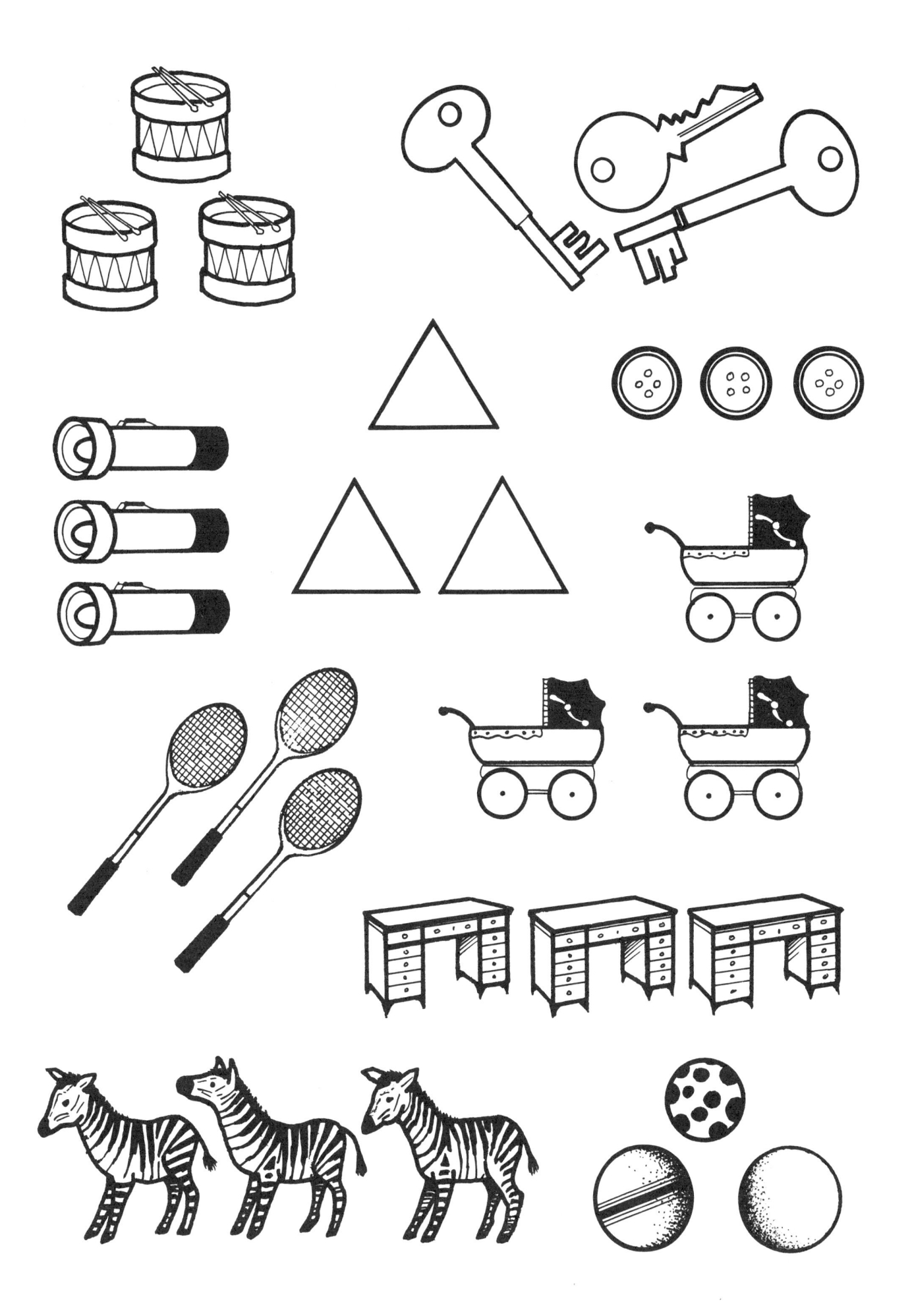

39

40 Colour the sets that have three (3) members

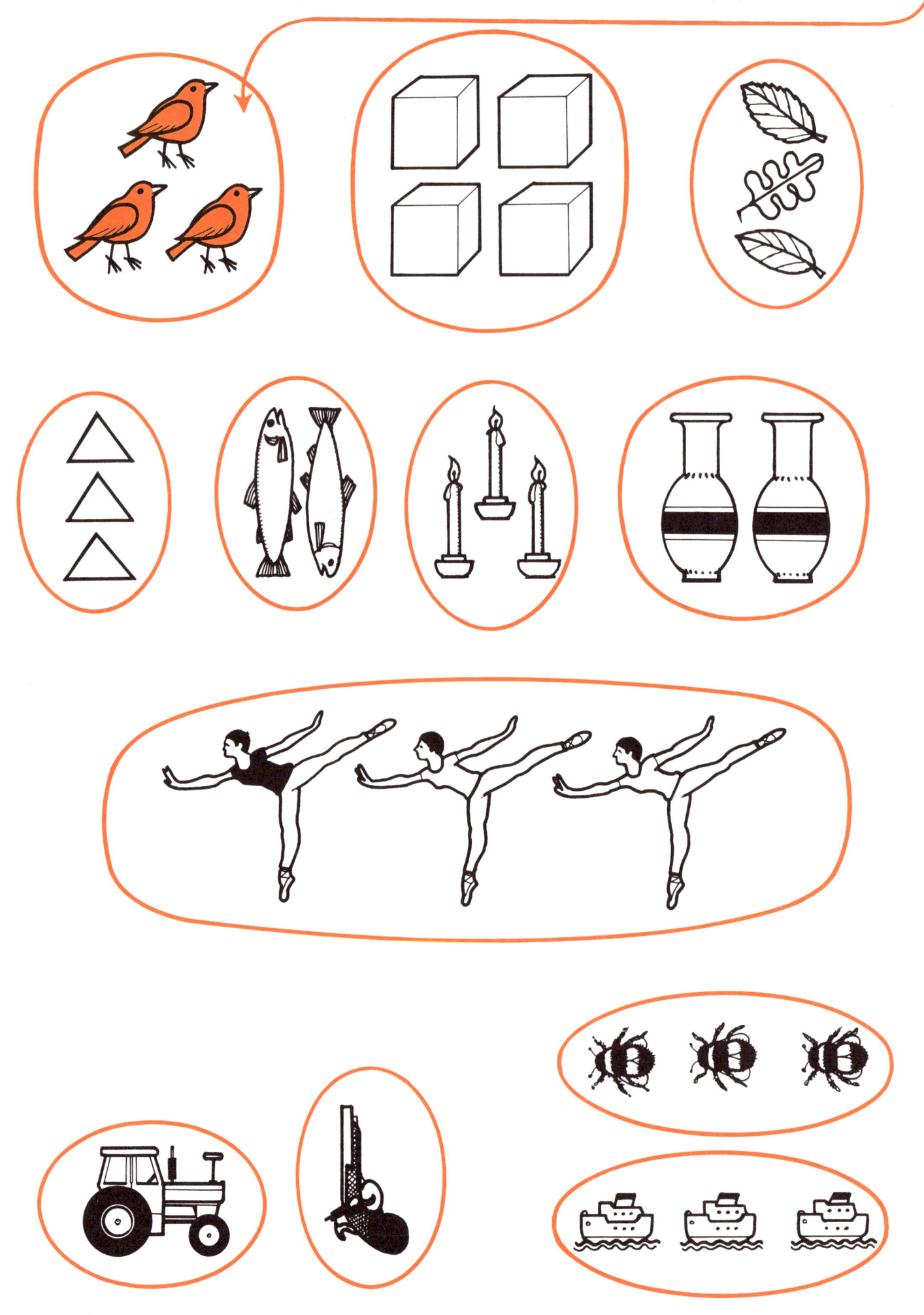

Colour the sets that have three (3) members. 41

42 Make each set into a set of three (3).

Make each set into a set of three (3). 43

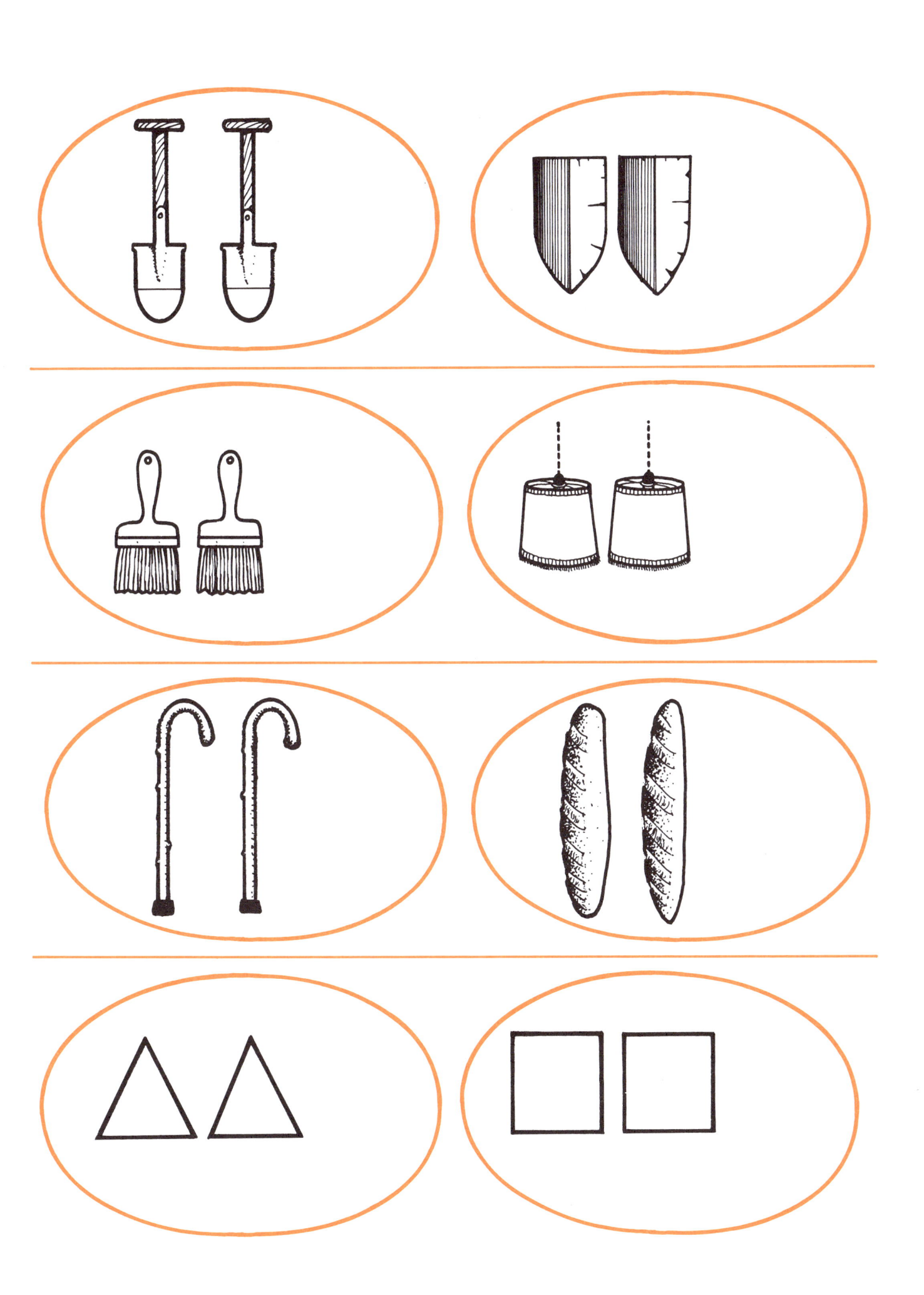

44 Colour the sets.   Write the numerals.

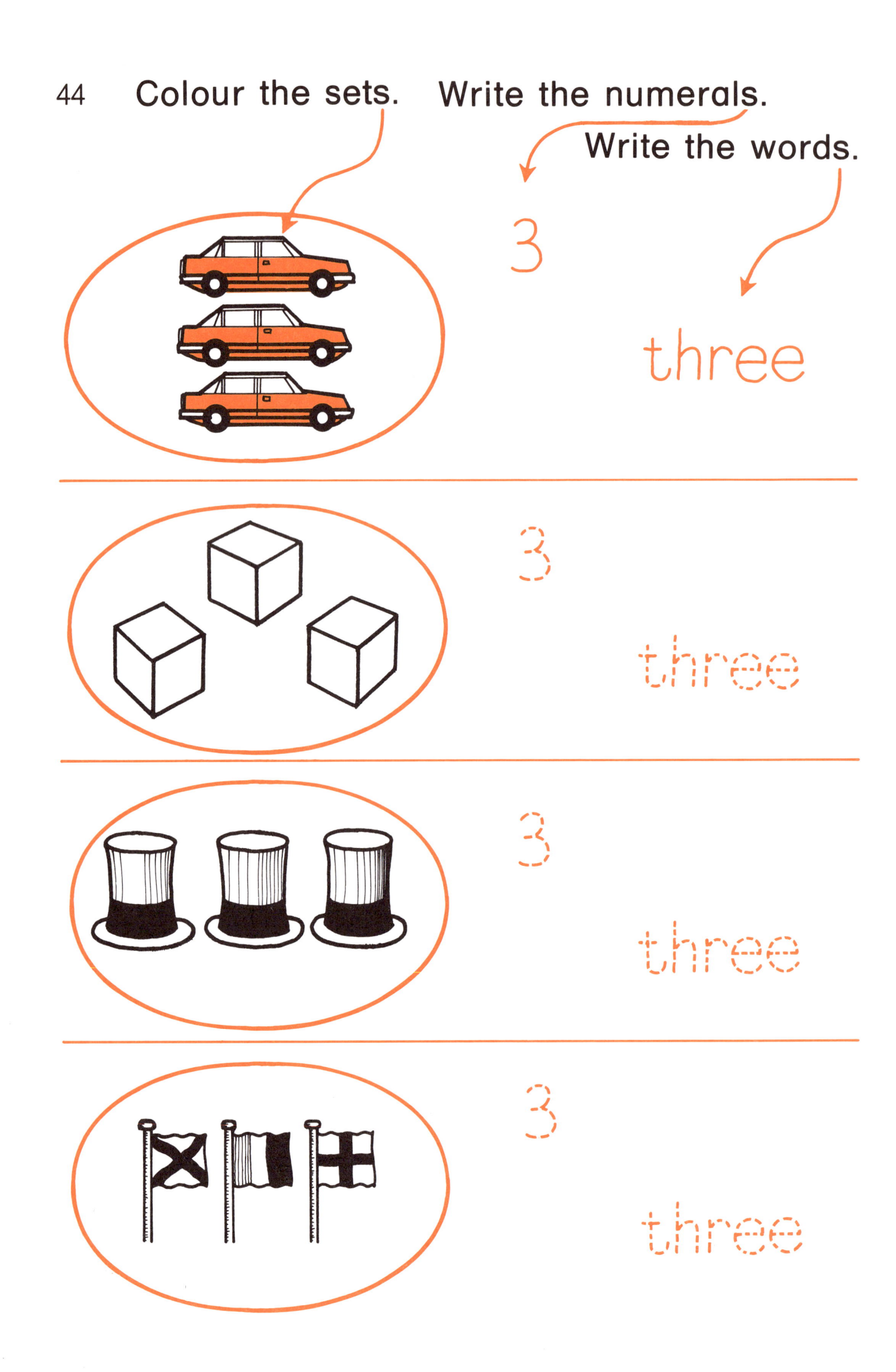

Write the words.

3

three

3

three

3

three

3

three

Colour the sets. Write the numerals.

Write the words.

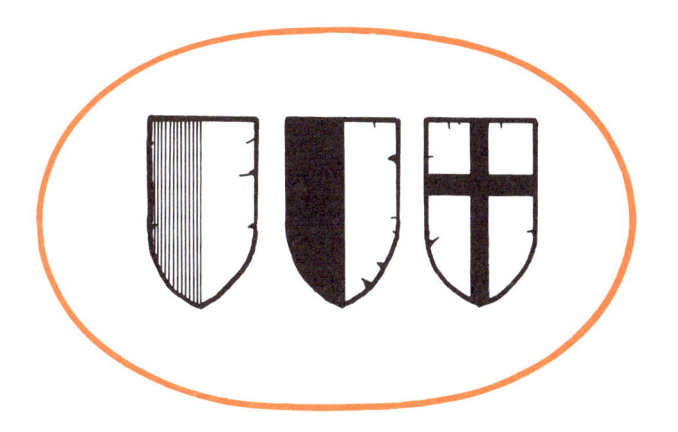

3 three

Oxford Introductory Maths Workbooks is a series designed to provide a gradual introduction to basic mathematical ideas, principles and language. Beginning at the pre-counting stage, the material focuses on the arrangement of familiar objects to lay the foundations of a real understanding of notation and what numbers mean.

This knowledge and awareness is then built on in order to bring out certain fundamental features of our number system – its additive nature, base, place value, conservation and reversibility and an understanding of the meaning and importance of zero. Throughout the course the material is presented in such a way as to encourage the pupils to discover these important elements for themselves by extracting the essential mathematical ideas from the activities in which they are embedded.

Since words are an integral and necessary part of mathematics these are introduced right away, though in strictly limited numbers at first and with adequate repetition. (Books 1 and 2 together employ a total vocabulary of only 61 words.) Mathematically correct terms are used in preference to apparently simpler but less precise words which may have to be 'unlearned' and discarded later on.

Special features of this scheme are:

☆ A systematic build-up of concepts
☆ The combination of discovery methods with the need for practice of basic skills
☆ Gradual progression and transition from one item to the next
☆ Early work consists of colouring and drawing and single-word responses
☆ Provision of ample reinforcement and revision
☆ Workbook format and layout is used to guide pupils towards accuracy and orderly habits of setting out their work
☆ Use of a limited, controlled vocabulary
☆ Each double-page opening is one unit of work
☆ Generous use of illustrations, diagrams and charts
☆ Clear examples at every stage

book 1 ISBN 0 19 918145 4
book 2 ISBN 0 19 918146 2
book 3 ISBN 0 19 918147 0
book 4 ISBN 0 19 918148 9
book 5 ISBN 0 19 918153 5
book 6 ISBN 0 19 918154 3
book 7 ISBN 0 19 918155 1
book 8 ISBN 0 19 918156 X

Oxford University Press
© Oliver Gregory
ISBN 0 19 918145 4

ISBN 0-19-918145-4